TOWN & COUNTRY

For Karen Anna

OTHER BOOKS BY ALICE AND MARTIN PROVENSEN

An Owl and Three Pussycats

The Glorious Flight
A Caldecott Award Book

Shaker Lane

BOOKS ILLUSTRATED BY ALICE AND MARTIN PROVENSEN

A Visit to William Blake's Inn
by Nancy Willard — A Caldecott Honor Book

The Voyage of the Ludgate Hill
by Nancy Willard

BOOKS BY ALICE PROVENSEN

The Buck Stops Here

My Fellow Americans

Library of Congress Cataloging-in-Publication Data
Provensen, Alice.
Town & country/by Alice and Martin Provensen.
p.   cm.
"Browndeer Press"
Originally published: London: J. Cape, 1984.
Summary: Describes life in a big city and on a farm near a village.
ISBN 0-15-200182-4
1. Cities and towns — Juvenile literature.
2. Farms — Juvenile literature.
3. Villages — Juvenile literature.
[1. City and town life. 2. Farm life. 3. Villages.]
I. Provensen, Martin. II. Title. III. Title: Town and country.
HT119.P76   1994
307 — dc20   93-44749

ABCDE

Printed in Hong Kong

TOWN & COUNTRY

ALICE AND MARTIN PROVENSEN

BROWNDEER PRESS
HARCOURT BRACE & COMPANY
San Diego   *New York*   *London*

There are many places to live in the world. You might live in a tent in the desert or
in a bamboo hut on a South Seas island. You could even live in an igloo on an iceberg.
But most people who live in the Western world live in a town or in a house in the country.

They might live in a hamlet — which is smaller than a village, or a village — which is
smaller than a town, or a town — which is smaller than a city, or a city — which is BIG.
These tracks lead to a big city somewhere in the world.

In a big city, you may live in a furnished room
or a town house or a mansion,
but most people who live in a really big city
live in an apartment,
and almost everyone who visits a big city
stays at a hotel.

If you have a room at the top
and a window with a view,
you can see so many things!

You can see planes flying overhead
and pigeons on the windowsills.

You can see ships at the dock
and boats on the river.

You can see office buildings
and factory buildings
and clock towers and water towers
and cathedral steeples.

When you look down
you look down on hundreds of cars
and hundreds and thousands of people
in the streets.

People seem as small as toys and as busy as ants
when you look down on them
from really high up.

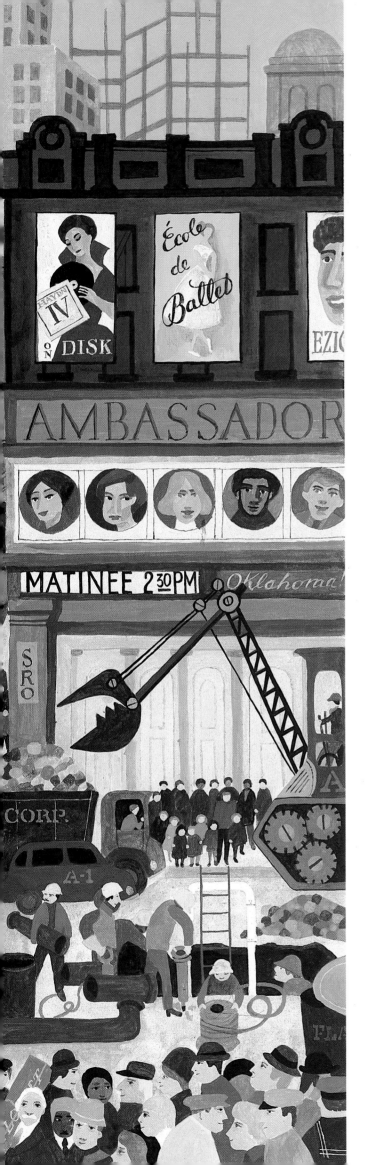

There is always something worth looking at
and listening to on the streets of a big city.
There are all those busy people! White people,
black people, tan people, big and little people,
fat and thin people coming and going,
walking fast, always in a hurry. You don't know
their names, but they look interesting.

There are big trucks and little taxis
and up- and downtown buses
with names and numbers.

Someone is always digging a hole in the pavement
with a pneumatic drill.
A building is being torn down.
Another is being built.
You can hear the blast of the dynamite.
You can see the trucks loading rubble,
and you can watch them unload concrete and cable
and plaster and plates of glass.

The police officers blow their whistles.
The cars rumble and rattle
as they change their gears to stop or go.

Sometimes a band marches by — a parade band
or a Salvation Army band with tamborines
and a big bass drum.

The whole city hums like a hive of bees.
It would be fun to spend all of your time
in the streets just looking and listening.

But children who live in the city
must go to school,
just like children everywhere.

You can walk to school if your school is close by.
If you are little, your parents may walk with you
on their way to work. Your mother or father
may be waiting for you when school is over.

Middle-size children are sometimes picked up
by a school bus and taken home again
after school.

Older children know how to get to school
and home again by themselves.

At a city school you learn the same things you
learn at any school, but at recess you go out to
play city games, either in the playground
or in the street in front of your school
if the traffic has been stopped
and the street is blocked off so it is safe.

There is not much space,
but there are lots of things to do during recess.
You can play hopscotch.
You can skateboard and roller-skate.
You can play jump rope.
You can play ball.

It is so crowded it is hard not to throw a ball
through a school window. If this happens
you not only make someone angry
but you will probably lose your ball.

On Saturdays and Sundays and holidays
you can go to the park to play.
In the park there is more space
than on the streets
and there are different things to do.

There is a lake with swans and ducks to
feed, and there are rowboats in the spring.
In winter there is an ice-skating rink
and a long hill for sledding.

Weather isn't very important in a city.
Rain or shine, hot or cold,
you can go to the zoo.
The library is open.
You can go to a museum,
to the aquarium, the planetarium,
or to a theater to see a play.

You can go shopping.
There are big department stores with
UP and DOWN escalators
and things to buy on every floor —
toys or clothes, or pots and pans.
In a very big city
some shops are open
twenty-four hours a day,
three hundred and sixty-five days a year.

BON MA

When you are hungry you can go out to eat
in a restaurant — any kind of restaurant:
an Indian restaurant, a Chinese restaurant,
or a French café.
There are Kosher restaurants
and fast-food restaurants
and salad bars and health-food cafeterias.

Would you like pancakes in a pancake house?
Would you like a pizza in a pizza parlor?
What about a nice hot cup of cocoa?

You can get any kind of food you want
in a city, and nothing is ever out of season.
You can get strawberries in November
and asparagus in January.

You can buy a pretzel from the pretzel lady
or a bag of hot roasted chestnuts
from the chestnut man on the streets
of a big city in December.

Not everyone lives in a tall building
in the tallest part of the city. In every city,
especially if it is old, there are neighborhoods
that are almost like small villages.

Here there are smaller houses and
small bakeries and butchers' shops
and fruit stands and flower stalls,
and people eat at home more often.

In an old neighborhood people know one another.
They greet each other on the street
and talk about the world and the baseball scores.
Some people even know your name.

There are curtains in the windows.
There are flowers in pots and boxes
on the windowsills. There might even be
a small backyard
where you could keep a puppy.

Sometimes there are block parties
or church bazaars
with banners and strings of lights
and balloons and games to play.
There are lotteries and shooting galleries
and fortune-tellers and food stands.

There is nothing that tastes as good as
a sizzling hot sausage with green peppers
cooked at a street-fair food stand!

When you go home to bed, you can still
see the lights and hear the sounds
from the neighboring street.

Even if your room
is on the top floor
of a big apartment house,
long after you are fast asleep
the lights of the city
will be shining on your ceiling.

A big city stays awake all night.
Neon signs blink on and off.
Traffic signals change from red to green.
Late buses stop or go.
Doormen whistle.
A taxi horn honks.

People are in the streets,
laughing and singing and shouting.

Far in the distance,
a siren answers a fire alarm.
A tugboat toots.
Underground, the trains rumble.

It is surprising how easy it is to sleep
through the sounds of a crowded city
if you are used to them.
But once in a while,
if you are wakeful,
you may imagine a subway
taking you out of the city
to a quiet place with lots of space.

A farm in the country is a quiet place with lots of space. Your nearest neighbor's house
may be a mile or more away. Though not so many people live here,
those who do will be good friends to you. Everyone will know your name.
And if there's no one around to talk to, there is always something worth looking at.

Beside your house there are barns and stables and toolsheds and tractor sheds.

There are fields and fences and streams and trees.

You can see an amazing amount of sky.

But a farm in the country is not quite as deserted and quiet as it seems.

Listen carefully.

Cows moo. Dogs bark. The sheep complain.

Cocks crow. Geese gabble. The cats meow. The tethered goat is bleating.

A combine whirrs and rattles.

A door slams. A shutter creaks. The wind gossips with the leaves.

You can feel the thunder in the distance.

You can hear the hay baler clank as the men hurry to bring in the hay before it rains.

Weather is important on a farm. Sometimes you need rain to make the seeds sprout.

Sometimes you need sun to make the crops grow. Sometimes it is too cold to go out

or too hot to stay in, but in any kind of weather there are things to do on a farm.

When the sky is gray and forbidding and the pond and streams are frozen, and the groun

To keep you warm, there is wood that can be brought in from the forest. With an early thaw there ar

If it is stormy, you can play in the hayloft of the big barn where it is quiet and warm and dry. Or yo

covered with snow, there are mile-long hills to slide down, ice-cold tracks to follow.

kes to fish and streams for boating. There is always an old farm dog who wants to play or walk with you.

an find an out-of-the-way place to read a good book while the rain drums on the windowpanes.

On school days, rain or shine, hot or cold, all the children who live in the country
must go to school, just like children everywhere.
The big children go to high school. The middle children go to the middle school.
The little children go to the elementary school at the edge of the village.
If you live on a farm a long way out in the country, you must be driven to school,
or there may be a school bus to pick you up. If you live nearer the village,
you can bicycle to school. The children who live in the village
walk to school by themselves.

At a village school you learn the same things you learn at a city school. You learn how to read and write and count. You may spend a little more time learning about farming and how to plant seeds out-of-doors instead of in window boxes, but you will also study art and music and history. You may take fewer museum trips and take more hiking trips, and at recess there is more than enough room to play.

There is room for hide and seek and games of tag.

There is space for basketball and volleyball and baseball and football.

If you lose a ball over the fence, only a cow may mind.

Some days your mother or father will pick you up after school if you have a dentist's appointment or you need new shoes. Then you have a chance to spend some time in the nearest small town. There is only one main street with shops, but it has a clothes shop and a variety store and a bank. You can buy candy or ice cream in the drugstore. Or you can buy a book in the bookstore. You can buy nails and paint and tools and string in the hardware shop.
Most of the food shopping is done in a supermarket, where you can buy coffee and tea and sugar or flour and oatmeal, or vanilla and cocoa and raisins, which don't grow on the farm.

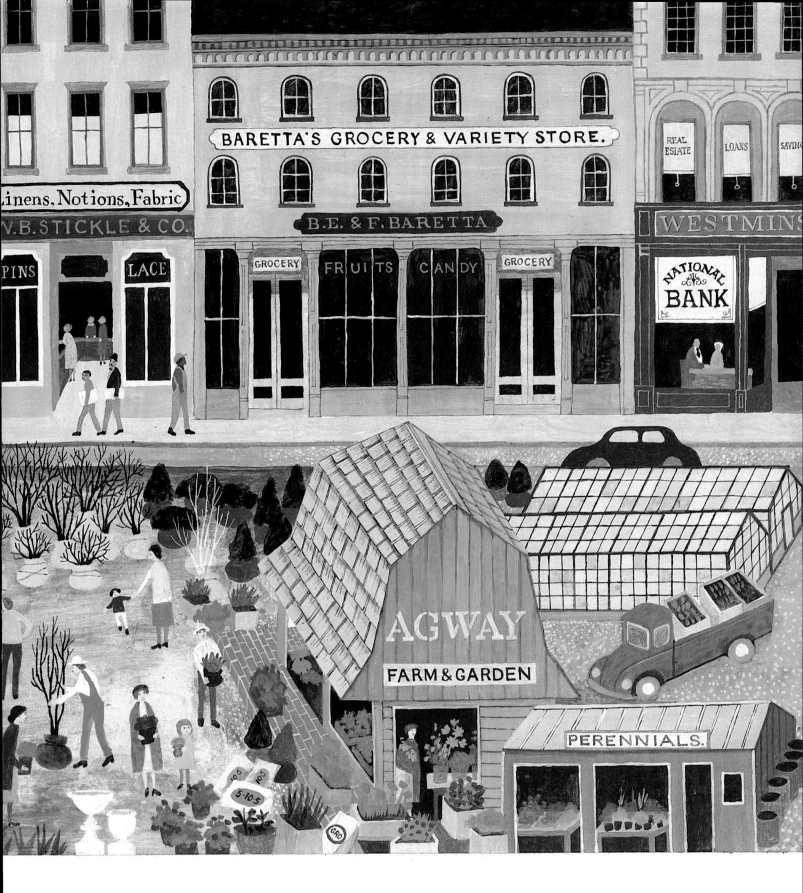

There are lots of things you do grow, though, like pears and apples and all kinds of vegetables.
You can buy vegetable seeds or seedlings from the nursery — lettuce and carrots and beans
and radishes, onions and cabbages and tomatoes. Everything tastes so good when it is fresh from
your garden! You can preserve your own vegetables in jars or in the freezer or make jam
from your own strawberries, and everything (with the possible exception of turnips)
tastes especially good because it is yours.

Digging, raking, planting, and weeding a garden is a lot of work, but it is worth it.

There is always work to be done on a farm. Older children help with the plowing and planting, the mowing, the haymaking, and the harvest. Fences need mending. Wood must be cut and stacked. The middle children bring in the cows in the evening and put out the hay. Even the little children help with the work on the farm.

You have to collect the eggs and feed and water the chickens.
(Be sure they are *all* locked up at night or they won't *all* be there in the morning!)
And all the farm work must be done before you even start your homework.
On a farm you are so tired at night you may doze over your books after dinner.

Once you are in bed, you can hardly stay awake long enough to say good night.
The lights are out early in the country.